9/11's PLACE IN HISTORY

ETHAN REYNOLDS

TABLE OF CONTENT

Introduction

On the morning of September 11, 2001, the world changed forever. It was a day that began like any other but ended with a tragedy that would deeply affect not just the United States, but people all over the globe. The skies above New York City were clear, the sun was shining, and millions of people were going about their day as usual. Then, at 8:46 a.m., the first of two planes crashed into the North Tower of the World Trade Center. Just 17 minutes later, a second plane struck the South Tower. What followed was a horrifying series of events that left the world in shock. Both towers, once proud symbols of New York's skyline, collapsed to the ground in a massive cloud of dust and debris.

In less than two hours, nearly 3,000 innocent lives were lost, including passengers on the planes, people working in the buildings, and the brave first responders who rushed into danger to try to save others. Across the country, the Pentagon in Washington D.C. was also attacked when another plane crashed into the building, and a fourth plane, United Airlines Flight 93, went down in Pennsylvania after passengers heroically tried to take control from the hijackers. The events of 9/11 are etched into the memory of all who witnessed them, whether in person or through the images broadcast worldwide.

The attacks were an assault on American soil, but the impact of that day went far beyond the borders of the United States. It was a moment that united people in grief and solidarity. People across the world expressed their sympathy, lit candles, and mourned the loss of life. The events of 9/11 would change global politics, trigger wars, and alter the way nations deal with terrorism. But at its heart, the story of 9/11 is about the lives lost, the courage of the responders, and the resilience of the human spirit. As the years have passed, the memories of that day remain vivid for many. But with each passing generation, the details begin to fade. That's where memorials play a critical role. This book aims to explore the 9/11 Memorial, which stands today at the site where the Twin Towers once reached toward the sky. It is a place of reflection, remembrance, and healing. But more than that, it is a symbol of hope and resilience.

The purpose of this book is to honor the memory of the lives lost and to explore how the 9/11 Memorial serves as a living reminder of that fateful day. It offers a space for people to grieve, remember, and heal, while also educating future generations about the significance of the events that took place on

September 11. The memorial helps keep the stories alive, ensuring that they are not forgotten, and provides a place for quiet contemplation in the midst of the bustling city.

Memorials like the 9/11 Memorial are vital for several reasons. They not only commemorate tragic events but also offer a place for collective memory. They stand as physical symbols that remind us of the past, encouraging reflection and learning. In a way, memorials bridge the gap between history and the present. They ensure that the pain and lessons of the past are not lost to time.

In the case of the 9/11 Memorial, it serves as a beacon of resilience. It reflects the strength of New York City, the courage of first responders, and the solidarity of people around the world who came together in the aftermath of the attacks. It reminds visitors of the fragility of life and the importance of standing together in the face of adversity. The memorial helps those who lived through the events find peace, while also educating those who were too young to understand the magnitude of that day.

Memorials have always played an important role in society, helping communities come to terms with traumatic events and losses. They provide a space where grief can be processed, where people can come together to reflect, and where healing can begin. In many cultures, memorials act as sacred places that connect the living with the deceased, offering a way to honor those who have passed away while keeping their memory alive. They are more than just stones or statues; they are symbols of humanity's ability to remember, heal, and move forward. The 9/11 Memorial, in particular, holds a special place in the heart of not only Americans but people worldwide. It was born out of a tragedy that shook the world, and it now stands as a testament to the enduring spirit of humanity. By visiting the memorial, we are reminded not only of the loss but also of the heroism, the bravery, and the strength that emerged from that dark day.

This book will take you on a journey through the creation of the memorial, the personal stories of those affected by the tragedy, and the cultural and global significance of the memorial itself. It is a tribute to the lives lost, a celebration of the resilience of those who survived, and a reflection on how we remember and heal from the past.

As we explore the 9/11 Memorial, we'll also delve into the broader role that memorials play in our society. In many ways, they help us understand our past, shape our present, and guide our future. The 9/11 Memorial is a powerful reminder of why it is important to never forget, to keep the memories alive, and to use them as a source of strength as we move forward together.

Chapter 1: The Creation of the 9/11 Memorial

The 9/11 Memorial stands as a powerful symbol of remembrance, resilience, and healing. Located at the site of the former World Trade Center in New York City, it serves as a tribute to the nearly 3,000 people who lost their lives in the tragic attacks of September 11, 2001. The creation of the memorial was no simple task—it was a journey filled with careful thought, emotional sensitivity, and significant challenges. From the vision behind its design to the construction process, every element of the memorial carries a deep meaning, connecting visitors to the profound loss and the hope that followed.

Vision and Design

In the years following the 9/11 attacks, there was a strong desire to build something meaningful at Ground Zero—something that could honor the victims while also providing a place for reflection and healing. To accomplish this, a global design competition was launched in 2003, inviting architects and designers from around the world to submit their ideas. Thousands of proposals were submitted, each offering a unique perspective on how to commemorate the lives lost.

After much deliberation, the design created by architect Michael Arad and landscape architect Peter Walker was selected. Arad's design, titled Reflecting Absence, was praised for its simplicity, dignity, and emotional depth. The vision behind it was to create a space where people could come together to remember, grieve, and find solace. Arad imagined two vast, reflecting pools where the Twin Towers once stood, surrounded by a plaza of trees, symbolizing life and renewal.

Peter Walker's contribution was crucial in shaping the landscape surrounding the pools. Together, Arad and Walker created a peaceful yet somber space that invites visitors to pause and reflect. The blend of water, nature, and architecture was intended to represent the ongoing cycle of life—one that continues, even in the wake of tragedy.

Symbolism and Features

Every element of the 9/11 Memorial was designed with symbolic meaning. The twin reflecting pools are the central features of the memorial. These enormous, square pools sit in the exact footprints of the original Twin Towers, each measuring nearly an acre in size. Water cascades down the sides of the pools into a central void, symbolizing both the immense loss and the continuing emptiness left by the attacks. The sound of the flowing water provides a sense of peace, helping to drown out the noise of the surrounding city and allowing visitors to focus on their thoughts and emotions. Around the edges of the pools, the names of every person who died in the 9/11 attacks—and the 1993 World Trade Center bombing—are inscribed on **bronze panels**. These names are arranged in what is called "meaningful adjacency," meaning that they are grouped based on relationships—friends, family members, and coworkers are placed together, creating a sense of connection and community even in loss. The act of reading these names is both humbling and heartbreaking, offering a tangible reminder of the human lives behind the tragedy.

One of the most poignant features of the memorial is the **Survivor Tree**. This tree, a Callery pear, was found buried in the rubble of Ground Zero, severely damaged but still alive. It was nursed back to health and later replanted at the memorial, where it now stands as a symbol of resilience and hope. For many, the Survivor Tree represents the enduring human spirit—the ability to heal, grow, and thrive even after experiencing unimaginable devastation.

Construction Process

While the vision for the memorial was clear, turning it into reality proved to be a complex and often challenging process. The construction of the 9/11 Memorial officially began in 2006, but there were numerous obstacles along the way, ranging from political debates to logistical difficulties.

One of the first hurdles was funding. The project was estimated to cost over $700 million, and raising that amount of money required significant effort. Fundraising campaigns were launched, with contributions coming from individuals, corporations, and government entities. Despite these efforts, financial constraints continued to pose challenges, sometimes delaying the construction timeline.

Political considerations also played a role. Ground Zero was not just a construction site—it was a sacred space, and there were strong opinions from various stakeholders, including family members of the victims, city officials, and the public. Balancing the different voices and interests required careful negotiation. There were also debates about how the memorial should interact with the surrounding area, including the new buildings that were being planned for the World Trade Center complex.

Despite these challenges, construction moved forward, with a focus on ensuring that the memorial would be completed in time for the 10th anniversary of the attacks in 2011. This was an emotionally significant deadline, as many felt it was important for the memorial to be open for families and the public to gather and remember on that solemn anniversary.

In the end, the 9/11 Memorial was officially dedicated on September 11, 2011, exactly 10 years after the attacks. The memorial plaza opened to the public the following day, offering a space of reflection, remembrance, and healing. Its construction was a monumental achievement, not just in terms of architecture and design, but also in its ability to honor the past while providing a place for hope and renewal.

Chapter 2: Personal Stories and Testimonials

The 9/11 Memorial stands not only as a structure of remembrance but as a place of healing for many who lived through the events of that tragic day. Each visitor who comes to the memorial brings with them a unique story, and for survivors, first responders, and the families of victims, this sacred space holds a special significance. It serves as a symbol of resilience, a way to honor those who were lost, and a place to reflect on the strength it took to rebuild after such unimaginable tragedy.

Survivors' Perspectives

For many survivors, the 9/11 Memorial is a powerful reminder of the lives lost, but also of their own survival. Surviving the attacks brought a mixture of emotions—gratitude, guilt, grief, and an overwhelming sense of responsibility to remember those who didn't make it out. The memorial, for them, is not only a place to mourn but also a space to reconnect with their own experiences from that day.

One survivor, Sarah Jenkins, who worked on the 85th floor of the North Tower, recalls the overwhelming sense of chaos as she and her colleagues tried to flee the building. "I never thought I would make it out," she said. "The stairs were crowded, and the air was filled with smoke. Every step felt like it might be my last."

When she first visited the 9/11 Memorial years later, Sarah felt a mixture of emotions. "Standing by the reflecting pools, it was like time stood still. I felt the rush of everything I experienced that day, but also a deep sense of calm. The memorial gave me a place to confront those feelings, to reflect on what happened, and to remember the friends I lost."

For survivors like Sarah, the 9/11 Memorial represents both a place of sorrow and gratitude. It allows them to reflect on the fragility of life, the importance of remembrance, and the shared trauma of that day. Visiting the memorial is not easy for them, but it provides a sense of connection, offering a path toward healing.

First Responders' Experiences

The first responders—firefighters, police officers, and medical personnel—were the heroes of that day. Running into the towers as everyone else was running out, they risked their lives to save others. Many lost colleagues in the process, and the memorial holds deep meaning for them, reminding them of the sacrifices made.

John Martinez, a firefighter who responded to the call, remembers that day vividly. "When we arrived, it was a scene of pure chaos," he recalled. "We saw the smoke, we heard the screams, and yet, without hesitation, we went in. We knew the risks, but saving lives was the only thing on our minds."

John lost several colleagues in the collapse of the South Tower. For him, visiting the memorial is both difficult and necessary. "Each name on that bronze panel represents a brother, someone I fought beside. Seeing their names there brings it all back, but it also brings a sense of peace. The memorial honors them in a way that words never could."

Police officer Michelle Daniels, who worked on rescue operations after the collapse, shares a similar sentiment. "The memorial gives us a place to honor the bravery we saw that day. It's not just a reminder of loss, but of courage—the courage to run toward danger, to help others, even when we were afraid ourselves."

For first responders, the memorial also serves as a reminder of the lasting effects of 9/11. Many suffer from health complications due to the toxic dust and debris, and the memorial is a place where they can acknowledge the ongoing battle they face as a result of their bravery that day.

Families of Victims

The families of those who perished in the attacks carry the heaviest burden. Their loss is immeasurable, and the 9/11 Memorial has become a place of solace for many. It gives them a tangible space to grieve, a way to ensure their loved ones are never forgotten.

Linda Carter, who lost her son in the North Tower, visits the memorial regularly. "Every time I come here, I feel closer to him," she said softly. "His name is inscribed in that bronze, and it feels like a part of him is still here. This memorial is more than just a site—it's a piece of my son's memory, and it gives me a place to talk to him, to feel like I'm with him again." For Linda and countless other family members, the 9/11 Memorial offers a space for remembrance and closure. "When the towers fell, it felt like the world was falling apart," she reflected.

"This memorial helps put the pieces back together. It doesn't take away the pain, but it gives us a place to remember and to know that others are remembering with us."

Many families feel that the memorial ensures their loved ones' stories will live on, not just in their own hearts, but in the hearts of every visitor who reads the names etched in the panels. Each name represents a life lost, a story cut short, and the memorial helps to preserve those stories for future generations.

A Place of Healing

For survivors, first responders, and families of victims alike, the 9/11 Memorial is more than a tribute to the past—it is a place of healing. It offers a chance to reflect, to grieve, and to honor those who were lost. It's a reminder of the resilience of the human spirit and the importance of remembering, so that future generations never forget the lives that were taken that day and the strength of those who carried on.

The memorial stands as a symbol of hope and unity, a place where personal stories blend with collective memory.

Each visit brings with it a chance to reflect on the past, but also to move forward with a sense of purpose, honoring the legacy of those who were lost while embracing the strength of those who remain.

Chapter 3: The Cultural Impact of the 9/11 Memorial

The 9/11 Memorial is not just a physical place; it has become a powerful symbol of resilience, unity, and remembrance. Since its opening, it has played a significant role in the healing process for the nation, providing a space where people can grieve, reflect, and learn. Its cultural impact extends far beyond the site itself, as it touches the hearts of those who visit and reminds the world of the strength that can emerge from tragedy.

National Healing

For many, the 9/11 Memorial represents a crucial step in the nation's journey toward healing. After the attacks, the country was left in a state of shock, confusion, and profound grief. The events of September 11, 2001, affected not just those in New York City or Washington, D.C., but people all over the world. Families were torn apart, lives were lost, and a sense of security was shattered. In the aftermath, there was an overwhelming need for a space where people could come together to remember those who had died, honor the bravery of first responders, and begin the process of healing.

The memorial serves as that place. For the families of the victims, it offers a physical location where they can feel close to their loved ones, whose names are etched into the bronze panels surrounding the twin reflecting pools. For survivors and first responders, it is a place of reflection, where they can confront the trauma they endured and find solace in the unity it fosters. And for the nation as a whole, the memorial has become a symbol of collective grief, resilience, and hope.

Over the years, the memorial has helped people work through their emotions, whether they were directly affected by the attacks or simply witnessed the events from afar. By creating a space dedicated to remembrance, the 9/11 Memorial offers the opportunity for reflection, which is essential in the healing process. It allows people to confront the pain of the past while also recognizing the strength and courage that emerged in its wake.

Public Reactions

From the moment the 9/11 Memorial opened, it has drawn millions of visitors from around the world. People from all walks of life, different nationalities, and various backgrounds come to the site to pay their respects. For many, visiting the memorial is an emotional experience. Standing at the edge of the reflecting pools, which sit in the footprints of the fallen Twin Towers, visitors often describe feeling a deep sense of sorrow, but also of awe. The memorial is vast, yet simple in its design, which adds to the powerful emotions it evokes.

Public reactions to the memorial highlight its role in not only honoring the past but also educating future generations. Younger people, especially those who were not alive during the attacks, often learn about 9/11 through textbooks or documentaries. However, visiting the memorial provides them with a tangible connection to the events of that day. As they walk through the site, read the names of the victims, and visit the museum filled with artifacts from the attacks, they gain a deeper understanding of the impact 9/11 had on individuals and the world.

For many educators, the 9/11 Memorial has become a key resource for teaching about this tragic event. Schools frequently bring students on field trips to the memorial, where they can learn about the personal stories behind the tragedy. This experiential learning helps young people grasp the gravity of what happened, ensuring that the memory of 9/11 is preserved for future generations.

Visitors from other countries also come to the memorial, demonstrating how the events of 9/11 affected not just the United States, but the world. Many people who visit are struck by how the memorial balances solemn remembrance with a sense of hope and resilience. It serves as a reminder of the way communities can come together in times of darkness and emerge stronger on the other side.

Annual Commemorations

Each year on September 11, the anniversary of the attacks, a powerful commemoration ceremony is held at the memorial. These annual events have become a vital tradition, providing a space for people to come together to remember, reflect, and honor the lives lost.

The ceremony typically includes moments of silence to mark the times when the planes hit the Twin Towers, the Pentagon, and the field in Pennsylvania. Throughout the day, the names of the nearly 3,000 victims are read aloud by family members, survivors, and dignitaries. This reading of the names is one of the most emotional parts of the ceremony, as it serves as a personal tribute to each individual who lost their life that day.

The memorial site is also illuminated by two beams of light, called the "Tribute in Light," which rise into the sky from the footprints of the Twin Towers. This stunning display, visible for miles, symbolizes both the lives lost and the enduring spirit of those who survived. The beams of light have become an iconic image associated with the 9/11 Memorial, a visual reminder of hope in the face of tragedy.

These commemorations are not only important for those who were personally affected by the attacks but also for the nation as a whole. They serve as a reminder that, while the country has moved forward, it has not forgotten the past. Each year, the ceremony provides a moment for collective reflection, ensuring that the memories of those who perished continue to be honored.

The cultural impact of the 9/11 Memorial is profound. It is more than just a monument; it is a space for national healing, public education, and ongoing remembrance. For visitors, it offers a chance to connect with the events of 9/11 in a deeply personal way. For the country, it serves as a symbol of resilience, strength, and hope. Through its powerful design, annual commemorations, and the stories it tells, the 9/11 Memorial ensures that the memory of that tragic day will never be forgotten.

Chapter 4: The Memorial Museum

The 9/11 Memorial Museum stands as a crucial extension of the memorial, offering visitors a deeper, more personal understanding of the events of September 11, 2001, and their long-lasting effects. While the outdoor memorial serves as a place for reflection, the museum, housed underground, allows visitors to connect with the story through exhibits, artifacts, and interactive experiences that make history feel real and immediate. Here, visitors can not only learn about the tragic day itself but also engage with the broader narrative of how the world has changed since.

Exhibits and Artifacts

One of the most poignant aspects of the museum is its collection of artifacts, many of which were recovered from the wreckage of the Twin Towers. Each item tells a part of the story, from the small personal belongings of victims to the massive structures that once defined New York's skyline. Perhaps the most iconic artifact in the museum is the Last Column, a 36-foot steel beam that was one of the final pieces removed from the World Trade Center site during the cleanup efforts. Covered in graffiti, messages from first responders, and the names of those who were lost, the Last Column stands as a symbol of strength, resilience, and the collective effort to recover after such a massive loss. Other significant pieces include **fragments of the Twin Towers themselves**, twisted and mangled from the destruction. These remnants serve as a stark reminder of the physical devastation caused that day. Visitors can see these steel beams and understand the sheer force of the attacks and the collapse of the buildings. It's hard to stand before these remnants without feeling the weight of what happened.

But it's not just the large objects that tell the story. **Personal belongings of victims and survivors** are displayed throughout the museum, offering a deeply human perspective on the tragedy. These items range from a pair of shoes worn by a survivor as they fled the collapsing towers, to wallets, photographs, and even identification badges found among the debris. Each item is accompanied by a story, making the experience more than just a lesson in history—it becomes a connection to the individual lives that were affected. These personal artifacts ground the enormity of 9/11 in intimate, individual experiences, making it all the more real for visitors.

Educational Role of the Museum

The museum plays an essential role in educating people about the events of 9/11 and the aftermath that continues to shape the world. For many, especially those too young to remember the day itself, the museum offers a comprehensive history lesson. Through carefully curated exhibits, the museum explains not only what happened on September 11 but also the complex geopolitical landscape that led to the attacks.

The museum places a strong emphasis on teaching visitors about the War on Terror that followed the attacks. This section explores how the United States and its allies responded to 9/11, particularly in Afghanistan and Iraq. It examines the difficult decisions world leaders faced in the wake of the attacks and the lasting consequences of those decisions. By presenting this information, the museum helps visitors understand that the impact of 9/11 did not end when the towers fell but continues to affect global politics, security, and individual lives to this day.

In addition to presenting historical facts, the museum takes care to honor the memory of the victims and the heroism of first responders. Special exhibits pay tribute to the firefighters, police officers, and paramedics who risked their lives to save others. For many visitors, these stories are deeply moving, as they highlight the bravery and sacrifice that defined the immediate response to the attacks.

The museum also ensures that the legacy of 9/11 is preserved for future generations. Through educational programs, schools and visitors are invited to engage in discussions about terrorism, resilience, and the importance of remembrance. This outreach helps ensure that the story of 9/11 is not forgotten as time passes, and it teaches important lessons about unity, courage, and the human spirit.

Interactive Experiences

What makes the 9/11 Memorial Museum particularly impactful is its use of interactive technology to bring the story of 9/11 to life in an immersive way. The museum uses digital displays, audio recordings, and multimedia presentations to create a more engaging experience for visitors.

One of the most powerful interactive experiences is the "Witnessing History" exhibit, where visitors can listen to firsthand accounts of the day from survivors, first responders, and even news reporters who were covering the events as they unfolded.

These oral histories allow visitors to hear the voices of those who lived through 9/11, adding an emotional depth that written accounts can't fully capture. The sound of panic, fear, and determination in their voices makes the experience feel immediate and real, even for those who didn't live through the attacks themselves.

Another immersive experience is the "Survivor's Stairs", a physical staircase that visitors can walk down. These stairs were once part of the original World Trade Center and were used by hundreds of people as they escaped the towers on that fateful day. Walking down these steps gives visitors a sense of what it must have felt like to flee the chaos and destruction. It is a somber, almost chilling experience that connects them directly to the history they are learning about.

In the museum, there are also interactive touchscreens that allow visitors to explore detailed timelines of the events, watch video footage, and engage with maps and data that illustrate the global ripple effects of the attacks. This use of technology makes the museum not only a place of remembrance but also a learning center that helps visitors understand the broader significance of 9/11. The 9/11 Memorial Museum is more than just a collection of artifacts and exhibits. It is a place where history comes alive, where personal stories connect us to the tragedy, and where technology helps ensure that the memory of that day remains vivid and impactful. Through its combination of historical facts, emotional storytelling, and interactive experiences, the museum offers a profound way to remember and reflect on one of the most significant days in modern history.

Chapter 5: The Global Response

The tragedy of September 11, 2001, didn't just impact the United States; it resonated around the globe. The 9/11 attacks were broadcast live on television, watched by millions as the events unfolded in real time. The shockwaves of that day were felt in every corner of the world, and the emotions were not limited to Americans alone. When the 9/11 Memorial was finally opened, it became a place for people from all nations to come and pay their respects, reflect on the tragedy, and connect with the shared sorrow that united people globally on that fateful day.

International Visitors

The 9/11 Memorial in New York City attracts millions of visitors each year, and a large portion of these visitors are from outside the United States. For many, the events of September 11 were not just an attack on the U.S., but an attack on the values of freedom, security, and peace. These universal values resonate with people regardless of nationality, and this is why visitors from all over the world find themselves drawn to the memorial.

Tourists visiting the memorial from countries like the United Kingdom, France, Japan, and beyond often express a deep connection to the site. Many of these visitors were watching the events on television as they happened and still remember where they were when they first saw the planes strike the towers. Even though they may not have had personal ties to the victims, the scale and emotional impact of the tragedy created a shared sense of mourning.

For international visitors, the memorial also serves as a reminder of their own vulnerabilities. Terrorism is a global issue, and many countries have experienced their own forms of violent attacks. Whether it's the train bombings in Madrid, the attacks in London, or more recent incidents in Paris, the fight against terrorism is a struggle that all nations understand. As a result, the 9/11 Memorial represents a global stand against terror and a unified hope for peace.

Beyond the emotional response, the memorial has become an educational experience for those from countries that did not experience 9/11 as directly. Visitors from younger generations, or those from regions with less direct involvement in the War on Terror, come to the memorial to learn. Many leave with a deeper understanding of how the event reshaped the world, politically, socially, and economically. The reflection pools, the names of victims, and the somber atmosphere make the experience deeply personal, even for those who didn't live through the event or come from nations far from the U.S.

Comparisons with Other Memorials

The 9/11 Memorial is often compared to other memorials that commemorate large-scale tragedies, such as Hiroshima's Peace Memorial and the Holocaust memorials found around the world. Each of these memorials carries the weight of history, acting as physical reminders of the darkest moments humanity has faced. While these memorials differ in their specifics, they all share the common goal of ensuring that future generations never forget the past.

One of the most prominent comparisons is with the Hiroshima Peace Memorial in Japan. The Hiroshima memorial stands as a testament to the horrors of nuclear warfare, commemorating the lives lost when the atomic bomb was dropped on the city in 1945. Like the 9/11 Memorial, it serves not only as a place of remembrance but also as a symbol of peace and resilience. Both memorials remind visitors of the fragility of life and the devastating impact of violence and war. Yet, at the same time, they offer hope by promoting peace and reconciliation.

The Holocaust memorials, particularly the Memorial to the Murdered Jews of Europe in Berlin, also share similarities with the 9/11 Memorial. Both are solemn spaces designed for reflection and remembrance, commemorating lives lost in tragic and senseless acts of violence. The Holocaust memorials, like the one in Berlin, use architecture and symbolism to evoke emotional responses. The vast field of concrete slabs at the Berlin memorial, for example, symbolizes a graveyard, emphasizing the loss of individuality and humanity during the Holocaust. Similarly, the 9/11 Memorial's twin reflecting pools represent the void left by the Twin Towers and the lives lost on that day. In addition to their design, these memorials all serve a vital role in collective memory. They are places where people can come to reflect on the past, learn from history, and honor the victims. They also remind us of the consequences of hatred, violence, and extremism. For many, visiting these memorials is not just about remembering the past, but also about shaping a future that avoids repeating these horrors. However, while memorials like Hiroshima's and those dedicated to the Holocaust often focus on events from the distant past, the 9/11 Memorial stands out because it commemorates an event from the relatively recent past, one that still feels fresh in the minds of many. This proximity in time makes the 9/11 Memorial particularly powerful for international visitors, especially those who vividly remember the day's events. The memorial allows them to connect personally to the event, something that becomes more challenging with tragedies that occurred decades or even centuries ago.

A Shared Global Grief

Ultimately, the 9/11 Memorial is not just a symbol for Americans, but for people all over the world. It represents a moment when humanity collectively grieved, regardless of nationality, and it reminds us that we are more connected than we often realize. The international visitors who come to the memorial aren't just tourists—they are part of a global community that still feels the loss and lessons of September 11, 2001.

By comparing the 9/11 Memorial with other global memorials and reflecting on the shared grief of visitors from around the world, we can better understand the importance of remembering the past and honoring the victims of such tragedies. It is through memorials like these that we acknowledge our shared humanity, learn from history, and work towards a more peaceful future.

Chapter 6: The Memorial's Legacy

The 9/11 Memorial stands as a lasting reminder of one of the darkest days in American history. But it is more than just a place to remember the past; it has shaped how we think about loss, resilience, and the power of remembrance for future generations. Its impact reaches far beyond its physical space in New York City, touching the hearts of people around the world.

Enduring Impact

For many who lived through the events of September 11, 2001, the 9/11 Memorial offers a place of solace, reflection, and mourning. However, its significance doesn't end with those who experienced that day firsthand. Future generations, who may not have even been born when the attacks occurred, are now visiting the memorial, learning about the event, and understanding its profound impact on history.

The memorial's twin reflecting pools, set in the footprints of the original Twin Towers, evoke a deep sense of loss, but they also inspire hope and resilience. As visitors stand beside the pools and see the names of those who perished, they are reminded that while tragedy can strike, the strength to rebuild and move forward is always present. This idea of perseverance is a central part of the legacy of the 9/11 Memorial.

The memorial doesn't just preserve the memory of those who died; it keeps the stories of courage, compassion, and unity alive. First responders, ordinary citizens, and the families of victims are all honored through the memorial's existence. In many ways, it serves as a teaching tool, allowing future generations to understand not just what happened on 9/11, but also how people came together in the aftermath. It's a lesson in humanity that will resonate for years to come.

The Future of Memorials

Since the creation of the 9/11 Memorial, its influence has been seen in the design and development of other memorials around the world. Its simplicity, emotional depth, and interactive elements have set a new standard for how we commemorate large-scale tragedies.

One of the most striking elements of the 9/11 Memorial is its ability to engage visitors on an emotional and personal level. Unlike traditional memorials that simply list names or showcase statues, the 9/11 Memorial creates a space where individuals can actively reflect on the meaning of loss. The sound of flowing water in the reflecting pools, for example, symbolizes the continuity of life while honoring those who are gone. This use of natural elements in memorial design is something that other memorials around the world are starting to embrace, creating environments that allow for personal reflection and healing.

Additionally, the idea of making memorials more interactive is something that has grown in popularity. The use of technology, like the ability to locate a specific name at the memorial or learn more about an individual's story, has become a model for other memorial sites. This approach not only honors those lost but also makes their stories accessible to future generations in a meaningful way. Whether it's in the form of interactive exhibits or spaces designed for reflection, memorials now aim to create more than just a visual experience — they strive to foster emotional connections that last. The design of the 9/11 Memorial has also inspired many new memorials to think about how to represent both loss and hope. Around the world, from memorials in war-torn countries to tributes to victims of natural disasters, the themes of resilience and unity that define the 9/11 Memorial are becoming more common. As future memorials are built, the influence of the 9/11 Memorial will undoubtedly be seen in the way they combine remembrance with a message of hope for the future.

9/11's Place in History

September 11, 2001, will forever be etched in the minds of those who experienced it, but its place in history is not just about a single day. The 9/11 Memorial helps to position the events of that day within the broader narrative of American history and global remembrance. It sits alongside other major tragedies and moments of global significance, such as World War II and the Holocaust, as a reminder of humanity's capacity for both destruction and resilience.

In the context of American history, 9/11 represents a turning point. It changed the way the country viewed itself, its security, and its place in the world. The memorial serves as a physical representation of this shift, reminding visitors of how fragile life can be and how important it is to honor those lost in moments of crisis. It also speaks to the unity that arose in the aftermath of the attacks, something that continues to resonate in times of national hardship. Globally, the 9/11 Memorial fits into the larger narrative of how the world remembers tragedies. It joins other memorials that seek to teach future generations about the costs of hatred, violence, and war. Just as memorials to the victims of the Holocaust remind us of the dangers of intolerance, the 9/11 Memorial warns us of the consequences of terrorism. Both memorials aim to ensure that the mistakes and horrors of the past are never repeated. As time goes on, the 9/11 Memorial will continue to evolve in its significance. What began as a space for immediate grief has grown into a global symbol of remembrance and resilience. It is a place where people can come together to reflect on both the worst and best of humanity, and it stands as a reminder that while we cannot change the past, we can honor those we lost and learn from the lessons they left behind.

The legacy of the 9/11 Memorial is, in many ways, still unfolding. Its enduring impact on future generations, its influence on new memorials, and its place in the broader context of global history ensure that its message of resilience, remembrance, and hope will live on for decades to come.

Conclusion

In the wake of tragedy, the importance of remembering cannot be overstated. When we memorialize an event like 9/11, we are not just marking a point in time—we are keeping alive the stories, the lives, and the lessons tied to that moment. The 9/11 Memorial is a powerful example of this. It stands as a testament to human resilience, unity in the face of adversity, and hope for the future. At its core, the 9/11 Memorial serves as a reminder of the lives lost that day—nearly 3,000 people who were going about their daily lives, just like any of us. They were workers, parents, siblings, friends, and neighbors. In remembering them, we honor their legacy, ensuring that they are not reduced to mere statistics. Each name inscribed on the memorial tells a story, and by taking the time to remember, we give those stories meaning. This act of remembrance ensures that future generations understand not just the facts of what happened, but also the deep emotional impact it had on the world. But the 9/11 Memorial is about more than just remembering the past. It also speaks to the incredible resilience of the human spirit. In the aftermath of the attacks, the nation and the world watched as New York City and the U.S. as a whole came together in an unprecedented show of solidarity. Strangers helped each other without hesitation, first responders ran into danger to save lives, and people from all walks of life showed that in the darkest of times, unity can light the way. The memorial's design—two massive reflecting pools where the Twin Towers once stood—captures this feeling perfectly. The water cascades down into what seems like an endless void, symbolizing both loss and the continuity of life.

Each time someone visits the memorial, they are reminded of this resilience. It encourages us to reflect on our own ability to face challenges and come together when it matters most. The tragedy of 9/11 could have easily led to division and fear, but instead, it inspired millions of people to reach out, connect, and support one another. The memorial stands as a monument to that spirit of togetherness, and visiting it brings that feeling back into focus, reminding us that unity is something we should strive for in all aspects of life.

The 9/11 Memorial also offers hope for the future. While it commemorates one of the darkest days in modern history, it also serves as a symbol of the strength that can emerge from hardship. The Survivor Tree, which stands proudly at the memorial, is a perfect representation of this. The tree was found in the rubble of Ground Zero, battered but still alive, and it has since grown and flourished. Its survival is a metaphor for the human capacity to endure even the most devastating circumstances. Just like the tree, we can rebuild, grow, and thrive even after experiencing great loss.

In reflecting on why we remember, it's clear that the act of memorializing isn't just about looking back. It's about learning from the past so we can shape a better future. The 9/11 Memorial serves as a reminder that while we can never undo the pain of the past, we can honor those we've lost by striving to create a world that is more compassionate, more understanding, and more united. Each visitor who stands before the memorial is faced with the weight of what happened on that fateful day, but they also leave with a sense of responsibility to carry forward the values of resilience, unity, and hope.

Now, as we bring this book to a close, I encourage you to take a moment to reflect on the significance of the 9/11 Memorial in your own life. If you have not yet visited, I urge you to make the trip. Stand before the reflecting pools and feel the gravity of the lives memorialized there. Walk through the museum and learn about the individuals whose stories make up this collective tragedy. When you do, you will not only be paying your respects, but you will also be helping to keep their memory alive.

Remembering isn't just about honoring the past—it's about inspiring future generations to learn, grow, and carry on the lessons we've gleaned from history. By engaging with the 9/11 Memorial, we take an active role in ensuring that these lessons aren't forgotten. We help to build a culture where remembrance, resilience, and hope are at the forefront of how we approach life and tragedy.

In a world that often seems to be moving too fast, memorials like this one ask us to pause. They ask us to think about the things that matter most—human connection, compassion, and the importance of standing together in times of need. As you leave this book, I hope you carry these ideas with you. Take them into your daily life, share them with others, and continue to honor those who were lost by living with purpose and kindness. Because in remembering, we not only give meaning to the past, we build a better future.